Cobwebs

ANJANA ARAVIND

First published in 2018 by

Becomeshakespeare.com
Wordit Content Design & Editing Services Pvt Ltd
Unit - 26, Building A-1, Nr Wadala RTO, Wadala (East),
Mumbai 400037, India
T:+91 8080226699

This book has been funded by WORDIT ART FUND
WORDIT ART FUND helps deserving
Authors publish their work
To apply for funding, please visit us at
becomeshakespeare.com

Copyright © Anjana Aravind 2018
All rights reserved. No part of this publication may
be reproduced, transmitted or stored in a retrieval
system in any form by any means, electronic, mechanical,
photocopying, recording or otherwise, without the prior
permission of the publisher

©
ISBN : 978-93-87649-14-9

To my beloved father,
Late **Shri Aravindakshan Nair**
Who first walked me through the world of words.

Acknowledgements

In life, there comes a moment of truth when one has to face the irrationalities that make or break them. Mine made me a better person. All credit to the singular irrationality that I cherish most.

To Seetharam, Ammu & Appu - My greatest source of support.

To my mom, brother, sister & her family, who painted my canvas bright.

To Chari Sir, the word smith, my mentor, whose gentle nudge made this book a reality.

To the editorial teams of Leadstart Publishing, Wordit Art Fund & becomeshakespear.com

To all my inspirations – known & unknown.

The lady of the forest green, Anjana, was born and brought up in the quaint and peaceful Aranmula – the abode of Parthasarathy by the river Pampa. Her inspiration is the nature in its grandeur of interior Kerala. She makes human figures & thoughts seem to evolve out of and pass back into this very landscape.

Anjana currently resides in Cochin with her husband and two lovely kids.

Contents

Author's Note 1

1. The Word Traveler 3
2. Vigil 4
3. Farewell 6
4. Resurrection 8
5. Fairy Tales 9
6. Palette 10
7. A Small Piece of Evening Sky 11
8. If only 12
9. Quarrels 13
10. Realistic 15
11. Grandmother's story 17
12. I will not sing a song about you 18
13. Bad 20
14. Synergy 22
15. Lost 23
16. It is raining again 24
17. When Rivers Rage 26
18. Cobwebs 28
19. So Called Friend 30
20. Traffic 32

21.	Travesty	34
22.	Mirror	36
23.	Dreams	37
24.	It Happened Thus	39
25.	Marionettes	41
26.	Silent Nights	43
27.	Barriers	44
28.	Crossroads	46
29.	Truth and nothing but the truth	49
30.	Yesterday I Flew over the Rose Garden	50

Author's Note

"I live in poetry. Blessed to have been born in a beautiful temple town, poems have been my constant companion. During beautiful summer afternoons, lying on the verandah of my home, listening to the chirping of birds, or watching the beauty of the night rain through the small window of the bedroom, every sound formed music and every word churned a poem in my mind.

Here is my little pot of nectar. Hope you enjoy it.

Love,
Anjana

1 - The Word Traveler

One was enough, I know now
But I spoke ten.
A whisper would have done it, sure,
But then, I shouted.
My pen needn't have written volumes
A word was all that mattered.

Yes, I, the word traveler,
Find it now, at the end of my journey,
The wisdom of silence.

2 - Vigil

The waves and shores embrace in final adieu
But unable to leave, the waves comeback
Yearning to stay, but shattering in little bubbles
The cries echoing throughout the shores
The sky mourning the demise of Sun
Veiled in black, sans decorations.

Trees swinging in the harsh wind
Cry in vain, branches breaking
And birds all nesting sheltered
Beneath the shadows, shivering.

The wrath of God about to strike
A streak of silver flashing
Across the ominous night.

The man sat in the little cabin
The wooden walls vibrating
And the roof tiles all rattling
His stare fixed on the narrow road
Watching, carefully.

The lone sentry in that forsaken land
Who bears the weight of the village in his soul
Who keeps the faith of people in his eyes.
Mingled with fear as dark as the night.
He starts singing, in low monotone
The stories of the warrior prince,
Who fought wars of lands and hearts
And won, sometimes and lost sometimes.

The song echoes through the village
Wind whistling in tune
The voice broken and shivering
Merging with the rain.

The man sat in the little cabin
The wooden walls vibrating
And the roof tiles all rattling
His stare fixed on the narrow road
Watching, carefully.

3 - Farewell

The raindrop never cried
Just before it left
The comfort of the clouds
To fall down and break

The water never fainted
When flowing down the river
Never to see the shores again
To vanish in to the sea

The music didn't break
When leaving from the flute
Wandering, sweet and soft
And dissolving in the air

The breeze never shivered
While caressing the leaves
One last time before moving past
Never to come back again.

Then why is it so?
That my eyes water, and
My heart break and I feel
This is the last day on Earth
When I am leaving you.

I will not cry, never.

4 - Resurrection

Withered and fallen, fused within the folds of earth
The beauty of ancient times, the memories, slept.

Still, always, the rain kissed seeds sprouted,
From their eternal trance, bringing life anew,
Flowering, the dance of life and death.

> *"In all things there is a law of cycles."*
> *Publius Cornelius Tacitus (55-117) Roman historian.*

5 - Fairy Tales

The hourglass figure is gone, much like a sack of potato now,
Vision is blurred, sound muffled,
White has its place even on my mighty head,
The love of my life, is mowing someone else's front lawn.
Like broken twigs in a torrential rain, we float.
Ephemeral visions of what it would have been, if…….
Come up, well, there are infinite ways to be jealous.

It is all, or nothing, I used to think once,
Prince Charming and glass slippers, of course,
The dance never ended, clock didn't strike midnight,
And all were well, then ah!!! Life struck.

The road I took was different, pathways tough,
The hand which held me close, unfamiliar.
The song we heard was of a new tune,
And the garden we passed, devastated.

I do not remember the words now –except, that,
"And then, they lived happily ever after."

6 - Palette

Swish!!!!!!!!!!!!! Swish!!!!!!!!!!!!!!!!!!
Brush strokes on a broken tile
Random colours merging
And my little daughter looks up at me
And laugh, with starry eyes.
The palette of life is full
All bright colours.

7 - A Small Piece of Evening Sky

It was mine, all mine, the small piece of evening sky,
Where the clouds played hide and seek,
The dark ones, the golden, and the grandfather whites.
Where the dancing twilight, with her star studded ensemble
Welcomed the moon with outstretched hands.

Gone are the times when I owned
That vast blue ocean of dreams
And the red lined clouds of desire and hope
Or an evening with just a cup of coffee
And sky unlimited.

8 - If only

Arrow piercing, blood pouring
Amid departed warriors
And moldering souls
Down by treacherous darts
Of love Gods
I look up, oh! My mother!

If only,
If only, you dunked my heart in Styx
Instead of my body
This pain of flesh I can suffer
But this pain of heart
That I can't.

(Remember the story of Achilles, the Greek hero)

9 - Quarrels

Lackadaisical words, shot likes arrows sharp
Pierced hearts, unexpected
And surrounded in obscurity
Fell down broken and spent
Starting rivers of blood, taking lives along.

Like wild forests which grew from the
Seeds thrown in careless abandon
The words multiplied, hidden hearts
Waited in silence to capture prey
Within the dark secrets.

Anchoring at the harbor of hate
The words brought storms
And turbulent waves
Which shook down the foundations
Of existence.

And then, and then,
When dawn broke, with beautiful sunbeams
Showering warmth, I looked for you

But, by then,
We were robbed of our ships and waters
Our words and our dreams
All capsized.

10 - Realistic

Mum's lullaby kept them safe
Through haphazard dreams.
One story a night was the promise.

Well, it was before you inherited this World.

Tuning the violin was passion, yester year's
Knife sharpening skills were not.
In that part of life, no dead babies washed up on the shores.
(Desperate calls for help never reached the net
But once dead, you are a star, a photo worth millions.)

Well, be realistic now!!!!
If you want to hear the love duets,
Or whispered sweet nothings,
This is the time to leave.

This is not the story of the knight in shining armor
Who sweeps the damsel in distress off her feet
And ride to happily ever after.

In this part of the story, the words are loud.

Masked robbers, chasing her dignity
And the heroes silently watching.
(The price of inaction, - well there is a famous quote,
Who cares if it is paid by another.)

This is not the story of eternal gardens
And blooming chrysanthemums
Through which, the couple walk hand in hand.

In this part of the story, the blooms are crushed.

Damsels disgraced, disfigured and killed.
They shed blood, not tears.
And then another story of glory begins:-
How they were brave to die
Well, where was the choice?

So my dear… No more fairy tales
And no more lullabies.
It will be war songs for you hereafter.

11 - Grandmother's story

"Between tears and more tears,
We bid adieu
It will not be the same again
May be in next birth, we have a chance
Now it is all over."

The question came popping, "Then what happened?"
Grandmother's eyes unseeing (or all seeing?)
Drifted from things to things, place to place
Her mind, already retired from life
But the faint smile continued.

And she said, "Life happened."

12 - I will not sing a song about you

Beyond the rose blooms, and the sweetest notes,
I am wise enough to see the thorns piercing,
And of course, flute is just a broken bamboo.

Pearled tears shine bright hiding the shadows in your smile
Gentle handshakes disguise the tremors of desperation
The calm and sweet words hide the vortex of pain

You are no conquering hero, in this battle of life.
Armor broken, blood pouring, soul bared,
You stand down, your chariot on fire.

Me the bard, watching alone,
Could see your eyes shine with hope, yet,
Of life and love and eternal peace.

Catching the torrent of sunbursts in a pot
And brewing Ambrosia in the labyrinths of hearts
You stand apart………….

No, I will not write a poem on you
Nor will I sing a song about you.

13 - Bad

None has promised me heaven yet,
But if they do I wouldn't go.

I do not have the ravenous desire to redeem myself,
I wouldn't know from what.
My eyes do not sift smiles showered my way
And my heart doesn't stifle feelings.
My feet cross the forbidden lines
And I do not follow the script.

World is a stage, the drama on.....
Act to the fullest, that's what I do.

Life… ha!!!!!

I do not mourn my lost dreams
Or pen elegy to memories
Can't help being the least favoured
Or Queen of hearts, its life.
It moves on floating
Like cotton wool on a countryside

Regrets, ha!!!!! ,

If only, I have more time to perfect being bad....
It feels so nice... so right.

14 - Synergy

Occasional silence broken by the messy bites of apples
Or the sporadic sips from a shared coffee mug

Sofa cover with food stains, the little toys scattered,
Battered remote, swapping channels
His screw drivers and my books
Sharing space in the same cupboard
The tableau of life is quite vivid.

Colours of my soul merge with his
Breathing the same air, singing the same tune,
In the alignment of our hearts
There is a rhythm, soft and sweet.
A kaleidoscope of love.

15 - Lost

Lost again, in these maze of life
Limping through the barricades
Indecision eats brain cells….
Breeding fear, colour blind
Hallucinating

It was only yesterday the Sun shone
Through the myriad pores
It was only yesterday the Violins played
The sweetest of songs

Between a shut eye and a dream
What happened?

War calls echo through the labyrinths
Blind rages play hide and seek
Nameless faces shout and rage
Lost again, in these maze of life

Between a shut eye and a dream
What happened?

16 - It is raining again

It's raining again.

Somewhere,
In the labyrinthine crossroads of my life
I stand troubled
Among strangers,
False promises,
And unwanted noise.

It's raining again.

Struggling hard to stay back
On the shivering banyan leaves
And failing, the raindrops
Shatter on the ground
The sound merging with
My heart beats.

Deep, fierce and shiny,
The new streams
Begin their journey.

And the fallen leaves
Drift aimless in the streams.

There was once,
Another cloud,
Another rain, at
Another place.
My beginning,
When my dreams were
Shapeless and colourless,
My eyes opened in to rain
Caressing the flowers
My first fragrance
With my mother's love.

Again,
On a sunny evening,
Love showering down my veins,
His lips on mine,
When our feathery dreams
Flew sky- high
I felt rain,
Soothing, soft and sweet.
It's raining again.
And like an idiot
I am smiling.
It's raining again.

17 - When Rivers Rage

In your eyes,
I saw the raging rivers
Twisting, turning, whirlpools of desire
Swallowing the little dreams
That vanished like
Broken twigs in a torrential flood.

Stormy, muddy and untamed
The power surge, which brew,
Thunders and storm…
Untold miseries and hurt.
The deceptive calm of
The deep waters
Forgotten blue of the hearts
Only the sound
Of the shattering waves
Reminded the rage
Unchained, inevitable.

It took everything,
Pulled in to the vortex

Of sorrow and then
When the lights died,
In to the sea of silent heartbreaks.
The ultimate resting place.

When rivers rage,
And storms gather,
The barriers break down
Thoughts, haphazard,
Flows down, and end
In the sea of silent heartbreaks.
The ultimate resting place.

It is but a season,
Short-lived.

18 - Cobwebs

Thoughts,
Brewing tastes in the morning
Knitting dreams in the afternoon
Occasional peeps of laughter,
Love and pain

An advice unaccepted
An unforgettable hug
A sweet memory
A lot of ideas and
A lazy attitude
Broken promises and tears

Rain trees shivering
In the cold breeze,
A sunflower,
A fallen banana tree,
And a withered garden
Neglected.

A jealous neighbor
A traffic jam
Treacherous kiss
Unsteady heartbeats

And,

I am prey, stranded
In these unbreakable cobwebs
Of love, laughter and despair
Waiting.

19 - So Called Friend

It is sad:-

I will always look for the thorn behind your soft petals now
You caught me unguarded once, you see
I will always read between your lines,
Since I found out the lies
I will always look for the traps beneath your smiles
You almost let me slip once
Now I know you are not a friend,
Your smile pains me
Your handshakes burn me
Displaying your love for me while you plotted behind my back
Lost within your own contradictions and one-upmanship
For temporary gains you lost a permanent friend
I feel a huge emptiness beyond pity
Of what a being you are…
Sleepless nights and scheming days
Eluding peace of mind.
Life is not a competition, why nobody told you that?

It is hard to return the smile you casually throw at me,
You are not my cross to bear, hence I forgive you.

20 - Traffic

Puddles, puddles, everywhere,
Confused lights, red or green?
Rain washing down painted faces,
Thoughts covered in plastics,
Like ants in haphazard order,
Life moves.

Puffing the poison in,
Deafening the ears,
Fighting, cursing and braking,
It goes on.

"You are what you have"
You pride on.
You just get entry
To where ever you want.

One can only wonder,
Watching from the sidelines,
Rush hour, or always?

Chances taken away,
Just swerve one way and there it goes.

It will all be gone one day,
No more roads to pass,
No more red, green or yellow,
No more dances of life,
Changing lanes.

21 - Travesty

It is not black and white anymore,
Do not try to read me,
Cocooned by this silence,
I want to rest.

A thousand smiles blind my eyes
A thousand words pain my ears
A thousand artificial beauties
Swarm my memory.

Haphazard thoughts,
Hug me close,
Too close that I suffocate,
Senses shut down, this moment,
Inside muffled walls of solitude
I feel the saddest.

You'll never see me cry,
You'll never see the wound
Your treacherous smile made in my heart,
Or the shattered fragments of my dreams.

Believe me, when the morning comes,
I'll be all sunshine and smile.
A beautiful vision to behold,
The sweetest word, ever heard.

22 - Mirror

Of the myriad memories lining my face
This is indelible
A matured hue shadows it, still,
I can see the outline
Of that chrysanthemum kiss we stole
On the first day of our forgotten bliss

And the pit on my cheek, not of pimples
But caused by the meteor tears I shed
When you were swinging like a pendulum
Between life and death on a hospital bed.

Endless worries of living, dreams deferred
And gone, shattered and scattered,
Line the whites of my once pretty forehead.
Gracefully though.

If you have nerve to look, the mirror shows it all.

23 - Dreams

Soft fluttering of wings
Splashed in multi-colours
A light heart
A smile
My dreams encircled me
Like butterflies
Whispering sweet nothings
It was morning and flowers
And sunshine then.

In my beauty sleep
among the chirping birds
and the comforting shades
Of mango trees
When the rivulet sung
Lullabies
I dreamt of babies
Playing in my backyard
Just after noon.

In the stone cold silence
When my bones chilled
When the tears froze
on my cheeks
I dreamt
of a bright red evening
and moonshine afterwards.
And cold wind blew.

Thunder raged
Lightning bolted
the night flooded with the
Darkest of everything
the rain broke down
All the defenses
and still I dreamt
It smelled of fear
And despair.

This moment I have no dreams.
No past, No future
I don't know what time it is.

24 - It Happened Thus

The Earth after the first rain
Smelled of long lost dreams
the rain drops falling from leaves
after a futile struggle,
made soft music out of its fall
vanishing in to the ground.
And the withered flowers
bled their heart in to the little streams
that went here and there.
I woke up in to the wet morning
And said, "What a nice day!"

I heard the music
But didn't see the falling rain drops
I put paper boats in to the streams
But didn't see the withered flowers
The smell of new rain, I felt,
But thought not of the dead clouds.

It was morning and I was awake.
And there were flower beds yet to bloom.

And Sun-rays to light up the life.
And a cool breeze to sooth me.

It happened thus, the beginning
of my new day.

25 - Marionettes

A small streak of red cloud
Framed the sky,
Like an isolated island
In the midst of a storm,
Fading, then, was the evening.
The stage was set, timing apt,
And marionettes danced.
Up and down, up and down,
Movements blurred.
Gloomy light, blinked on them
Reminding past so bright.
Fading faces, once loved,
Came and went so fast.
And marionettes danced.
Some one there, sure, pulls
The unseen strings,
Someone there, sure, sets
The unheard tunes.
Whose unseen hands

Make them dance?
Marionettes never think,
They only dance.

26 - Silent Nights

Music of dewdrops falling on rose petals,
Moonlit pathways where butterflies sleep,
Silent prayer of a nightjar,
Mist laden grass,
My nights are silent.

Shining stars in the clear sky
Echoing your heartbeats,
Wet breeze after the rain
Whispering sweet nothings,
My love infinite for you
Flowing through my veins
Like a wild rivulet,
All are there but
My nights are silent.

27 - Barriers

Partitioned and secured
Carefully guarded
This little piece of land
Sliced from the generous heart of love
You bound me within.

Love me till the moonlight ends
No more
Follow me till the guarded gate
Not further
Look, of course,
There is a window.
Touch me yes, but
Within these walls
Not further
Sing for me, only
The songs I want
And talk, only these words,
You told.

You gave me unlimited rules

Of love, life and sociality.
You defined words, languages
And expressions.

Let me tell you this my World

I love you beyond boundaries
I touch till my skin blend with yours
I sing till there is no song left
I talk till there is no voice left
I look till there is no view left
And I walk till there is nowhere to go

I want thunder, lightning
A storm to break the walls
A flood, rain to crumble the barriers
Unlimited sky and sunshine
Stars moon and wind
The extremes
I want everything.

28 - Crossroads

Whimpering rain clouds wandering above
The sleepy meadows and plains
Shedding occasional tears in the dark
And the barren road accepting
The sorrow in its red hot bosom
A blinking street lamp, peeping
And intruding in the silent union

And I stood there, at the crossroads
Thinking of history, repetitions and regrets
Chaste thoughts, intelligent dreams
And deep rooted beliefs
All these, of no use, vanish
The mind blank, cold and clear
The body shivering in the cold.

Should I think of the choices I have?
Which path to cross?
Or which to abandon?

I can see the flower beds
Waiting to bloom for me
When I pass
I can hear the lark
Singing for me
On the tree.
I can feel the winter,
The spring and the summer
Which I am to cross
I can see the tempest brewing
For me on the way.

I can also feel the songs
I won't hear
The blooms I won't see
The cold I won't feel
The summer and spring
And the tempest I won't have
On the roads I won't take

Or shall I think?
Of the choice
I don't have
To turn back the clock
Retract the steps
Take a different turn
Never to be here
Erase the summers and springs

And the winter I already had
Clear my eyes from
Sights I have seen
Empty my ears of the
Voices heard

How many more choices to make?
How many roads to take?
And how many people stood here,
Before me and chose?

29 - Truth and nothing but the truth

Let me tell you the truth, once and for all.
Traitor heart of my own, still before the fall.
I am no great poet, I can't write an epic
It is only a few lines, on some silly topic.
I do laugh, I do cry, I do it through my verses
I write for me, not for you, not for any praises.
Still, I do not mind, if you want to peep
Grab a smile, shed a tear, and take a word to keep.
My verses are like notes, from the heart of a flute
Which belongs to the World, after it is out.
You can't own it then, when you give it a form
You can only share words of eternal charm.

30 - Yesterday I Flew over the Rose Garden

Bowing my head and
Kneeling before you
Touching your feet
I ask your blessings, my world,
For, it is time to leave.
The untouched virgin lands
Are calling.

I remember the words
Of wisdom and love
You spoke.
I remember the laughs, the hugs
The rabbit chases and songs
I remember everything.
But, I have to go
It is time.

Yesterday,
I flew over the rose garden

Over the tiled roofs of the homes
Of unknown inhabitants
Over the silvery river which
Slices the land in two
And yesterday, I flew far beyond
The Banyan trees, the bordering
Gulmohars.

Spreading my wings
Exploring the far flung sky
Feeling the wind on my face
Drinking up the sunshine
Looking
Touching the horizon
Among the silver lined clouds
Yesterday, I flew over the rose garden.

And so,
I have to go
The unfelt fragrances are waiting
Other rivers, other flowers
Other horizons and forests
Are waiting.

www.ingramcontent.com/pod-product-compliance
Lightning Source LLC
Chambersburg PA
CBHW031430040426
42444CB00006B/759